Entrepreneurship:

Theories & Practices

Bryan Law LLD

Fox College of Business

First edition: January 2021

Fox College of Business

Disclaimer

Fox College of Business and Bryan Law are not engaged in rendering legal, accounting, real estate, or other professional services. This book should not be relied upon as providing such advice. We strongly urge that you seek professional advice prior to acting on the information contained herein.

The information contained herein has been obtained from sources which we believe are reliable, but we cannot guarantee its accuracy or completeness. Fox College of Business, Bryan Law, and every person involved in creating this book disclaim any warranty as to the accuracy, completeness, and currency of the contents of this book. We also disclaim all liability in respect of the results of any action taken or not taken in reliance upon information in this book.

Preface

As a business college professor, I have been involved in teaching different programs such as Accounting and Finance, Business Management, Commercial Tenancies, Contemporary Marketing, Entrepreneurship, Feng Shui Theories, Investment Analysis, and Legal Studies. Among them, Entrepreneurship is the subject that arouses the students' most interest and makes them ask most questions.

As an entrepreneur, I have established three corporations. I sold one of them, and the other two are running fine. They can be operated without my involvement. That is, I can sell them at any time, just like the first one. However, I still need a platform to try my business theories to prove or counter-prove them to my students.

As a management consultant, I have helped clients in different industries develop their businesses, reduce expenses, and streamline customer flows. Some of them are entrepreneurs. From them, I found out some of the entrepreneurs' challenges that were not obvious enough for people to be aware of them ahead of time.

Through the years, I have acquired the knowledge I needed from institutions and books and gained experience from my businesses. I shared them with my students and applied them in my businesses, and vice versa. There are too many topics to be discussed and too much information to be included in this book. I hope this book can provide all the concise and essential information to people who want to be entrepreneurs.

Bryan Law BSc (Pure Maths), LLM, LLD

A well-known author, consultant, educator and entrepreneur in Canada, Bryan has a diversified professional background.

Bryan is a management consultant with more than 20 years of experience. He is also a legal researcher in various areas, including contract law, environmental law, human rights law, labour law, privacy law, and real estate law.

Different education institutions have hired Bryan to provide his expertise in business management, law, and real estate. Bryan has authored over 20 books in various disciplines, including human rights, creative problem-solving, franchising, real estate, Feng Shui, employment law, and more.

Bryan's wide-ranging knowledge and professional experience, coupled with humorous presentation skills, have placed him in demand as a professional speaker as well.

Table of Contents

1. Introduction

We learn business concepts, models, techniques, and theories from institutions and books. The topics are rich, and the common subjects include marketing, selling, and management. They are all valuable knowledge that all business people rely on to do their jobs, make important decisions, run their business and develop their enterprises. However, most of us will only utilize a few areas of those subjects.

If you are an accountant, you will focus on accounting and finance, maybe management as well. If you are a marketing professional, you will not spend too much effort learning accounting and finance. However, entrepreneurs need to deal with most of the areas. They do not have to be experts in any of those fields, but they should have a basic understanding of them. Knowing the basics enables them to start their business correctly and efficiently. They also need particular knowledge to hire competent employees in the future.

What is Entrepreneurship?

According to the Merriam-Webster dictionary, an entrepreneur is:

One who organizes, manages, and assumes the risks of a business or enterprise. [1]

Oxford dictionary has a similar definition,[2] but the Cambridge dictionary defines an entrepreneur as:

Someone who starts their own business, especially when this involves seeing a new opportunity. [3]

The differences between the two are the words 'a new opportunity' and 'assumes the risks'. While Merriam-Webster emphasizes the assumption of risk by an entrepreneur, Cambridge stresses the importance of starting a new business opportunity.

---

[1] "entrepreneur", Merriam-Webster.com Dictionary, Merriam-Webster, last accessed September 20, 2023, https://www.merriam-webster.com/dictionary/entrepreneur

[2] "entrepreneur", Oxford Learner's Dictionaries, last accessed September 20, 2023, https://www.oxfordlearnersdictionaries.com/definition/english/entrepreneur

[3] "entrepreneur", Cambridge Dictionary, last accessed September 20, 2023, https://dictionary.cambridge.org/dictionary/english/entrepreneur

Investopedia has an extended definition that combines both definitions. It says,

> *An entrepreneur is an individual who creates a new business, bearing most of the risks and enjoying most of the rewards.* [4]

Interestingly, Wikipedia gives a more narrow definition, which is the longest among the four. It states that entrepreneurship is

> *the process of designing, launching and running a new business, which is often initially a small business, or as the "capacity and willingness to develop, organize and manage a business venture along with any of its risks to make a profit".* [5]

This definition fits the concept of 'entrepreneurship' in most people's minds. It detailly describes what has to be done by entrepreneurs – from designing to running the business, often a small business, with a willingness to develop it along with its risks.

---

[4] "entrepreneur", Investopedia, last accessed September 20, 2023,
https://www.investopedia.com/terms/e/entrepreneur.asp
[5] "Entrepreneurship", Wikipedia, last accessed September 20, 2023,
https://en.wikipedia.org/wiki/Entrepreneurship

Can you be an entrepreneur?

Since setting up and running a business involves risks, not every person can bear such risks. In general, the two main risks are losing your time and money.

Most entrepreneurs are young adults, and there are reasons behind it. First of all, one has to reach the legal age to hold a corporation if sole proprietorship and partnership are not options (the differences among different types of business structures will be discussed in Chapter 7). Secondly, an entrepreneur needs to spend more time and be more energetic, which may be a challenge for some people with a family or older people.

One of my students told me his case. Although it was about hiring him as a salesperson, the job's involvement and nature were more or less like those of an entrepreneur. He said the interviewer just asked him two questions. The first one was, "Are you married?"[6] The second question was, "Do you have a girlfriend?"[7] His answers to all questions were "No", and he was hired immediately.

He said the boss told him the rationale behind why she asked such questions after my student was hired – he would have no time to take care of his family and even have

---

[6] Raising such issues by an employer is against human rights law in Canada
[7] Ditto

no time to date. The student said she was right as he had to work from 7 a.m. to 11 p.m. every day after joining them, with no weekends and holidays off. Although he was making good money, he told me he was considering quitting to have a more balanced life.

The student's case was quite similar to the typical situation that entrepreneurs face, especially when the business has a limited budget, and the owner has to work in different roles in the company. Taking an entrepreneur's role means you may have to sacrifice the opportunities to accompany your family, meet with your friends, enjoy your free time, and even eat and sleep.

One of the examples of the most successful entrepreneurship is the creation of Apple Computer. When Apple was founded in 1976, initially, there were three partners – Steve Jobs, Steve Wozniak, and Ronald Wayne.[8] They formed a business partnership in which Wayne owned 10% of the newly founded company. He sold it back to Jobs and Wozniak for $800 only after 12 days.[9] Although Wayne did not tell exactly how demanding it was to be a partner of a tech startup, he once told the media, "If I had stayed with

---

[8] "Apple Inc.", Wikipedia, last accessed September 20, 2023, https://en.wikipedia.org/wiki/Apple_Inc.
[9] "Ronald Wayne", Wikipedia, last accessed September 20, 2023, https://en.wikipedia.org/wiki/Ronald_Wayne

them through the Apple corporation phase, I probably would have ended up the richest man in the cemetery."[10]

Financial risk is another thing that entrepreneurs have to consider. You may have to contribute the initial capital from your own savings or borrow from other sources (we will discuss this in Chapter 4). You may not have any cash flow generated from the business that you can use to pay your personal bills during the first few months or a few years. If the business venture eventually fails, you may end up losing all your capital, owing money to your creditor, or even worse, having to declare bankruptcy.

On the other hand, being an entrepreneur can give you flexibility. You can better manage your time, especially if you have good time management skills. Not all entrepreneurs put making money as their goal, at least not their only goal. Personal achievement is the top motivation of small business owners, with 37% of the surveyed business owners listed it as their ultimate goal. The second place is recognition, with 29% of the surveyed business owners saying that receiving an award is their proudest business moment. Financial stability ranked third, with 28% of the

---

[10] "Apple co-founder sold his shares for $800. Today they'd be worth $94 billion. He regrets nothing", Global News, April 14, 2019, https://globalnews.ca/news/5158415/apple-co-founder-ronald-wayne/

surveyed business owners using financial rewards to measure whether an entrepreneur is successful or not.[11]

There are other pros and cons to being an entrepreneur. However, it does not matter whether you like them or not; a prerequisite to running a successful business is your commitment. You must have the ambition to be a successful business owner and be prepared to sacrifice your time and risk your investment capital.

---

[11] "Money vs. Happiness: Manta-Dell Study Reveals Unique Insights Into Small Business Ownership and the Life of an Entrepreneur", Yahoo! Finance, last updated April 22, 2014, https://finance.yahoo.com/news/money-vs-happiness-manta-dell-130000985.html

2. Business Model

The first thing entrepreneurs have to do is to have an idea about what kind of business they will do. In other words, you have to have products or services to provide to your customers. The process of setting up your products or services to deliver them to your customers should be planned, although it will have to be modified along with the growth of your business.

Many people have great products or can provide satisfactory services, but they fail to be successful entrepreneurs. The reason is that they were unable to utilize their products or services to make money. A simple example is a parent who can make delicious hamburgers or sew beautiful shirts and pants, but they are just for the kids and are not for sale. As a result, the parents will not be successful entrepreneurs, even if the products or services are excellent, because their role is not entrepreneurs when providing those products and services.

Therefore, you need a business model to be an entrepreneur. Although it has many different definitions, a business model is simply a plan to make money using products or services.

Your Product

You have to have a product or service for your business model. Although we will discuss Marketing Mix[12] in Chapter Six, it is essential to talk about "Product" in this chapter.

In marketing, a product is a tangible object or an intangible one for sale. Intangible products are services based, including the transportation industry, hotel industry or insurance brokerages. Examples of tangible products are clothing, computers and pens. A product has to have its uniqueness to retain its competitiveness in the market. Product differentiation is required for a business to be successful as it is one of the strategies to stand out from its competitors.

The first question you have to ask yourself is, "What is my product?" Your product may be a new concept, a hi-tech one, or simply a traditional one, such as a restaurant. It does not matter what product it is; you must know your product well. We will talk about new concepts and hi-tech products in the next section. Now, let us consider the traditional product first.

---

[12] "Marketing mix", Wikipedia, last accessed September 20, 2023, https://en.wikipedia.org/wiki/Marketing_mix

A traditional product means something that already exists in the market, such as a coffee shop, a soft drink, or furniture. Since everyone knows what these products are, you do not have to introduce any new concepts to the consumers. However, there is no guarantee that your product has an excellent product-market fit. A product-market fit *is the degree to which a product satisfies a strong market demand.*[13]

A traditional product has a strong market, but it does not mean that your product fits the market well. For example, the furniture market has a revenue of more than $200 billion in the United States,[14] and you need only $1 million in revenue to make your company survive. Still, the high demand for furniture does not mean that the consumers will be interested in your furniture, and you may end up having a revenue far less than $1 million.

In a traditional market, it is difficult for new entrants to compete with the key players. That is exceptionally true when new entrants are small entrepreneurs and the key players are giants. For example, it is difficult for a small store to go into a price war with the big retailers as the big

---

[13] "Product/market fit", Wikipedia, last accessed September 20, 2023, https://en.wikipedia.org/wiki/Product/market_fit

[14] "Revenue of the furniture market worldwide by country in 2020", Statista, last accessed September 20, 2023, https://www.statista.com/forecasts/758621/revenue-of-the-furniture-market-worldwide-by-country

retailers have the absolute advantage of getting significant discounts from the suppliers due to their large quantity orders. New entrants will have to use different tactics to compete with the leaders. You have to have an edge to stand out from the competitors' products, such as a good design, a better function, or a higher cost performance.

It is the same for all other traditional products, such as a restaurant. If you are going to open a hamburger restaurant, how do you compete with the leaders such as McDonald's, Burger King and Wendy's? You have to have at least one thing that is an advantage over them. You have to ask yourself: Are my burgers more delicious? Is my restaurant more comfortable? Do I provide some special foods? Is my location more conveniently accessible?

Even if your answers are "yes" to all the above questions, you are still not sure that you can attract consumers, although the chances are much higher. On the other hand, some restaurants have huge success just because their foods are much cheaper than the competitors but nothing better. It depends on other factors that we will discuss in the following chapters.

We can consider two scenarios. The first one is that there is already a need for a particular product, and you make one to feed the demand. The second scenario is that you have a great product and want to use it to attract consumers. Traditional products belong to the former one, and new products and concepts belong to the latter one.

Is it Feasible?

It is an exciting moment when you get a brilliant idea for creating a new product. However, the first thing you have to do is to make sure that your idea is feasible. That is, it can be turned into a real product or supported by the existing technology or infrastructure.

Here is an analogy: Let's say you are an engineer and have drafted a blueprint for making a commercial supersonic jet. The blueprint is perfect in a way that everything is logical and possible. However, when you try to make it, you may find out that the existing manufacturing technology cannot produce precise measurements of your parts, and the materials cannot stand the extreme temperature when your engine is ignited. That means you cannot make the jet without having the necessary equipment, parts and materials.

Even if you can make the jet without any problem, your jet may not fit the requirements of commercial airports all over the world. Your jet may be too large to use their runways, or their runways are too short for your jet. In other words, your jet cannot be flown and thus has no market.

A product has to be feasible and accepted by the consumer. It does not matter how good your product is or how creative your idea is; if you cannot produce it or there is no market for it, your business venture will fail.

One way to tell if there is a market (a need) for your product is to know the consumers' pain points and then make sure your product can help the consumers deal with them. A pain point is a problem that prospective customers are experiencing. For example, a pain point for bicycle commuters may be that there is no space for them to park their bikes in the area around their office. A bike-sharing program with ample parking spaces may be the right product for that market.

Once you have a viable product that can take care of the consumers' pain points, you are one step closer to success. The next step is how to use it to make profits.

Profitable Business

Your business needs profits to survive. A company with a successful product and a high sales revenue does not necessarily mean that it is profitable.

Many companies tried their luck during the dot com fever about twenty years ago by offering online shopping experiences to consumers. Most of them failed because there were many challenges that business people had never faced before. Some of them closed their business for good, but some learned a lesson and reentered the field after a few years by revising and improving their business models.

The first challenge was the colour choice. When consumers saw the products on the computer screen, the product colours were not exactly the same as the real objects. Moreover, different monitors may produce different product colours. That was a severe problem in some industries, such as the garment industry. The product picked by the customers might not match their expectations, especially when they had to match with other clothing. As a result, many customers returned their products, and the company lost money in shipping and other logistic costs.

The difference in sizes was also an issue that caused many clothing companies to end their online stores. Unlike traditional retail stores, online stores have no fitting rooms to try on the clothing or feel the material's exact quality. Again, unsatisfied customers would return their products after receiving them.

For products like books, brand-named canned food and electronic products, they do not have the above problems. However, a company selling those products still ended up losing millions of money and had to close its online store after a few years.

That company spent a huge amount of money on advertising, and its logistic was not well-planned. Moreover, each product's profit margin was too low, as they were generic products that consumers could buy at any supermarket. Furthermore, it provided free delivery without a minimum purchase amount to attract people to use its service. As a result, it lost $20 per item sold online on average. The more items it sold, the more money it lost. What caused the problem was that the company did not have enough customers to cover its fixed costs, and its variable costs were also too high. The situation is like an airline providing low prize air tickets, but only one ticket is sold for every flight, so the airline loses money on every flight. The more flights it flies, the more money it loses.

The main issue is setting a profitable pricing strategy. It depends on the situation; there are different pricing strategies to set the price of a product. For example, jewellers and designers may set the prices of their products using the premium pricing strategy. A premium pricing strategy is a *practice of keeping the price of one of the products or services artificially high in order to encourage favourable perceptions among buyers based solely on the price.*[15]

---

[15] "Premium pricing", Wikipedia, last accessed September 20, 2023,
https://en.wikipedia.org/wiki/Premium_pricing

For example, you will be proud to tell your loved ones that you have spent $30,000 to buy a designer's ring, and they will probably look at your ring with envy. All of you may not question why a small ring could sell for such a high price. We will talk about price strategies again in the Marketing Mix in Chapter 6.

To succeed in your business venture, you need a detailed business model to plan how your company can profit from running the company. Do not set up a business just because you want to be an entrepreneur.

3.   Management

A business cannot be run without management. The entrepreneur is the management mastermind, but a bigger management team may be required, depending on the scale of the business. The fact is that a team can do things much faster than a person, and a team can bring broader knowledge and experience to the company than a single person.

Small Business Ownership

Most entrepreneurs started their businesses on a small scale, usually by themselves or with a team of not more than three people. There are advantages and disadvantages of such small business ownership.

Advantages

The first advantage is that you have better control of the business. You do not have to make decisions to satisfy a large number of shareholders. Your ideas do not need approval by the management because you are the management. That gives the second advantage – you can make a decision much faster due to the small management team and simple structure. In a large corporation, issues are reported from lower levels to the management. It takes time to change a corporation, especially when it involves significant changes such as corporate core business, value or culture.

As a small business owner, you will have the opportunity to learn and practice all the business skills. You can acquire different hands-on experience in various functions – P&L accountability, product development, strategy, finance, HR, sales, marketing and more. Those are valuable experiences and knowledge that every executive needs. When your business becomes successful, you can enjoy the financial rewards and freedom. Personal satisfaction is another benefit that you can gain from operating a small business.

Disadvantages

As the owner of a small business, you will have to spend much more time at work than when you were hired as an employee. Running a business is a time-consuming task, especially when it is a small one, and you are the sole owner. You will have to manage your time wisely; otherwise, you will be burnt out, and your health may also be affected. You will also have to deal with stress when managing your own business.

In addition to investing time, you will have to invest the money as well. That is the financial risk we talked about in Chapter 1. As the owner, you will have to take over some undesirable duties as well. You may have to be the receptionist, courier and janitor of your company. You may also have to learn and perform tasks that you do not know or do not like to do, such as accounting, selling, hiring people and terminating their employment.

Team Work

Building up a team for a business venture has several benefits. First of all, if the team members are also shareholders, the capital raised from shareholders will be more than that from the sole proprietor alone. The network of the management team is bigger than that of a sole entrepreneur alone, so it will be easier to raise capital from the outside (we will talk about how to get financing in Chapter 4). Secondly, a team spirit can motivate each other and cheer up the entrepreneurs' willpower, especially when the company's performance does not meet their expectations. Moreover, as we have mentioned above, a team can do things much faster than a person and bring broader knowledge and experience to the company.

Similar to Apple Inc, most successful business ventures have more than one entrepreneur when founded:

Google, Microsoft, Youtube, Facebook and more. Both Google and Microsoft started with two partners[16, 17] while Youtube has three founders,[18] and Facebook has five co-founders.[19]

All those tech startups were founded by entrepreneurs with technical backgrounds, or we should say computer backgrounds. Founders with technical knowledge is a must for tech startups. Entrepreneurs with technical backgrounds can turn their new ideas into reality without paying extra costs to hire professionals. However, technical persons may not be good managers, so they need to add people to their team with management expertise at a certain stage. Conversely, entrepreneurs who have only management skills and great ideas will have to team up with technical people to make sure that their product is feasible.

[16] "History of Google", Wikipedia, last accessed September 20, 2023,
https://en.wikipedia.org/wiki/History_of_Google
[17] "History of Microsoft", Wikipedia, last accessed September 20, 2023,
https://en.wikipedia.org/wiki/History_of_Microsoft
[18] "History of YouTube", Wikipedia, last accessed September 20, 2023,
https://en.wikipedia.org/wiki/History_of_YouTube
[19] "History of Facebook", Wikipedia, last accessed September 20, 2023,
https://en.wikipedia.org/wiki/History_of_Facebook

Building Your Team

Even if you are the only one who got the idea of having a business venture, you still need to build up your team sooner or later. Your team members may be entrepreneurs who are willing to bear the same kinds of risks as you do, and you all work as partners. All of you may have the same background, say, technical persons. It is also possible that some of you come from different backgrounds and complement each other.

Your team members can also be your employees. In this case, you may have a better opportunity to pick the members as the choice is not limited to the people you know. As a startup, your company may not compete with big corporations in salary and fringe benefits, but you can offer bonuses, shares or stock options as incentives in their employment.

It does not matter whether your management team members are partners or employees; their backgrounds have to be well-balanced. A tech firm should have not less than 50% of its management with technical backgrounds, but it cannot operate without a member with a management background, although key positions can be added after its infant stage.

Team building is not an easy task; even the most experienced human resources professionals may pick the wrong candidate. It depends on how the mismatch is made; sometimes, the wrongly selected employee and the company can be turned into a perfect match.

One of the cases was that a restaurant founder hired a lady as their Head of Operation. The lady had years of experience in a fast-food chain, but she was not familiar with the operation of that fusion-style, fine-dining restaurant. The owner found that she had a good work attitude and was knowledgeable in fast-food restaurants and chain operations, but she just could not blend in with his company. After analyzing the situation, the owner put her to assist the marketing and sales team. It turned out that was a very successful move as the lady knew different types of restaurants well and was able to help his restaurant stand out from the crowd.

However, that is one of a few fortunate cases for both the mismatched employee and employer. In most other cases, it might result in employment termination when the employee could not fit into the position.

Company Culture

A successful entrepreneur will establish a company culture for its business. It may be created at the early stage as the company's philosophy or established during its development and expansion. Good company culture helps the company keep its spirits and morals, which may also help the company gain a good reputation and public recognition.

The founders of the search engine giant Google set their corporate culture as "Don't be evil."[20] Advertisers' listings are distinguished from other listings by colour-coded or added words to indicate that they are the advertisements on their search engine. Therefore, the searcher can tell which are the results and which are the advertisements. Google even analyzes the advertisers to ensure that their content complies with Google's company policy that their websites are 'valuable' in Google's standard. Such a policy makes people feel much more comfortable using Google to search online.

On the other hand, another search engine giant, Baidu, did not have such a policy. It was involved in a scandal regarding a student who had sought medical treatment from a hospital that came top of the list on his Baidu web search and died. Baidu was under fire for allegedly selling listings to bidders without adequately

---

[20] "Don't be evil", Wikipedia, last accessed September 20, 2023, https://en.wikipedia.org/wiki/Don%27t_be_evil

checking their claims.[21] That caused Baidu to lose its reputation as well as the credibility of its search results.

The big three management consulting firms[22] have their own company cultures. Their approaches are classified by the clients and the public as aggressive, conservative, collaborative, hierarchical, fratty or harsh. Their employees know that well, too. Therefore, when there is a vacancy in a particular company, the interviewers can tell if an interviewee will be a good fit for their culture or not during the interview.

It is a good idea to have a company culture, as the corporation can use it as a cohesive force and give the employees a sense of belonging as people of the same type like to get together. However, if a company sets its culture too soon, such as during its infant stage, it may limit its growth.

For example, an entrepreneur may be risk-taking and willing to seize every opportunity; even such an opportunity may cost the company its entire capital. When such an entrepreneur sets up the management team, the company

[21] "China investigates search engine Baidu after student's death", Wikipedia, last updated May 3, 2016, https://www.bbc.com/news/business-36189252

[22] "Big Three (management consultancies)", Wikipedia, last accessed September 20, 2023, https://en.wikipedia.org/wiki/Big_Three_(management_consultancies)

culture may be a risk-taking spirit. The advantage of such a company culture is that the company is aggressive enough to have rapid development. The disadvantage is that a single failure may cost the company its entire capital and cause the business venture's termination.

On the other hand, a conservative company culture set up at its infant stage may hinder its growth.

4. Finance

As an entrepreneur, you need capital to make your great idea come true. It depends on what kind of ideas you have in mind – an online store, a mobile app, a retail store, a new fusion-style restaurant or a piece of innovative equipment. The capital you need ranges from a few hundred dollars to millions.

Your business venture can be a long-term project before a profit can be made. Saving the initial capital is one of the most challenging hurdles that an entrepreneur will have to overcome. We will start the financing options from a small amount, as low as hundreds of dollars, to a significant investment as high as multi-million dollars.

Saving Your Money

If you need just a few hundred or a thousand dollars, you may want to save the money yourself instead of borrowing it from a third party. Unless the lender is willing to lend you the money unconditionally, there is a risk that the lender may claim their interest in your company once your business venture becomes a successful one. That was why Steve Jobs and Steve Wozniak had to ask the third co-founder of Apple Computer to accept a US$1,500 to forfeit any potential future claims against the newly incorporated Apple Inc.[23]

If you need to save your capital investment from scratch, you should not overlook small savings. Small amounts of money carefully saved can quickly add up to large amounts to invest in your business venture. For example, did you know that over 2.25 billion cups of coffee are consumed in the world daily? More than 150 million adults drink coffee daily in the United States.[24] In 2020, all Americans drank an average of 1.87 cups of coffee per day.[25] With a total population of 328 million, it is fair to say that, on average, an American coffee drinker drinks about 1,493 cups of coffee every year.

If you are a coffee drinker, you may save some money on coffee drinks. Say you drink four cups every day, and two of them were bought in coffee shops. You can save $2 a day by storing your coffee in a thermal and bringing it to

[23] "Ronald Wayne", Wikipedia, last accessed September 20, 2023, https://en.wikipedia.org/wiki/Ronald_Wayne
[24] "Economics of coffee", Wikipedia, last accessed September 20, 2023, https://en.wikipedia.org/wiki/Economics_of_coffee
[25] "Total coffee per capita consumption in the United States from 2011 to 2020(in cups per day)", Statista Inc,)", last accessed September 20, 2023, https://www.statista.com/statistics/456360/total-us-coffee-per-capita-consumption/

work or brewing your coffee in your workplace and sharing the costs with your colleagues. That can save you more than $500 a year that you would spend by buying coffee in coffee shops and much more in luxury cafes.

A Part-Time Job

Around twenty years ago, my friend John worked for an engineering firm for three years after obtaining the Professional Engineer designation. His income at that time was $50,000 a year, and he lived by himself, but he had no money left in his pocket, not even a penny. He used the cash advance service provided by credit card companies to pay for his spending: vacations, a nice coupe, home theatre and all the luxuries. He knew it would lead him to bankruptcy sooner or later, but it was hard for him to change those spending habits. I suggested he find a part-time job and work both nights and weekends. He did and ultimately paid off all his debts in two years.

The benefit of a part-time job is more than earning extra money for you; you will have less chance to spend money, too. If your part-time job earns you $100 a week after tax, you may save more than $100 a week, as you will not have the time to spend. You may save over $10,000 a year; income tax has to be deducted, however.

It is not uncommon that some entrepreneurs have to do part-time jobs to supply on-going cash flows for their business venture. The main reason is that the new business may not produce any profit in the first year or two. Even if it can, the cash flow may not be good enough to pay your bills. A part-time job supply extra cash flows to both the business and yourself. Of course, the downside is that you cannot focus on your new venture and may have insufficient time to finish your work at your own company.

Money from Individuals

You may not be able to save the required capital within a short period of time, and the market will not wait for you. As a result, your innovative idea may become outdated over time. Therefore, you may have to use other people's money, from your parents, siblings, relatives or friends. You may be able to borrow money from them at a very low-interest rate or even at no interest. Try to divide the money you need into small amounts so that everyone can afford to lend it to you.

For example, if you need $10,000 as your capital, you should divide the $10,000 into $500 portions. Asking people to lend you $500 is much easier than asking them to lend you $2,000 or more. Moreover, people will seldom ask for interest for a $500 loan. Nevertheless, you should try your best to pay back such loans to them as soon as possible because they are your assets, and you may need their assistance in the future. Good reputation and credit history are always your number-one priorities.

You must sign an agreement with the lender or giver for the money received. The nature and the content of the agreements depend on your relationships with the lender or giver. If the money is given for natural love and affection, such as from your parents, the contract should state that the money is a gift and must be signed under seal. If the money is given as a loan, you should state whether it is interest-free or not and the date to be paid back. If the loan is interest-bearing, the agreement should spell out the interest rate and the payment schedule. It does not matter if the loan is amortized over a period or you will pay off the debt by a lump sum payment at the end; you have to tell how the interest will be calculated. It can be compounded monthly or yearly, or just a flat amount each year as simple interest. For a small loan, the interest rate is usually calculated by simple interest or compounded annually.

If the loan is a significant one, the lender may want to receive monthly or periodical repayments and amortize it over a few years (usually three to five years). You can use an online financial calculator to determine the payment amount and put it in the agreement. In all cases, you must indicate that the loan is not for buying any share or interest in your business, and the lender should have no right to make such claims.

In all cases, you must have a business plan to tell the lenders how you will profit from your business and, hence, pay back their money. The business plan does not have to be formal, but it helps the lenders understand how you will carry out your business plan so that they will have more confidence in your business. Sometimes, they may challenge your thoughts, which may have a positive impact on your venture, too.

Borrow from the Banks

You may apply for a business loan from the banks, use your house to arrange a mortgage or apply for a secured or unsecured line of credit. The money available may be more than the loans from individuals but less than from venture capital firms, which will be discussed in the next section.

You will have to draft a business proposal to apply for the loan and may have to show your personal and business net worth so the banks can judge your ability to repay your debt. The bank will look at your past credit history to gauge your creditability. You should have maintained a good credit history and a good credit rating;

otherwise, the banks will unlikely approve your loan application.

The banks may ask you to use your assets as collateral to secure the business loan. Some of those assets may be bought using the funds that you privately borrowed through family and friends. The banks will become the secured creditors of those assets instead of those who lent you the money to buy those assets.

Your total debts cannot exceed a certain level, including the business loan that the bank will lend you. That calculated ratio is called a Total Debt Service (TDS) ratio. If your TDS is too high, you may choose to pay off some of your existing debts to be qualified for this measure. If you have a partner, your borrowing power may be increased unless your partner has a poor credit record or a high TDS ratio.

Unlike mortgages, a business load does not have an amortization period as long as 25 or 30 years. Usually, you will have to pay off your loan in five years.

Venture Capital

If you have a brilliant idea, especially if it is related to information technology and services, you may not need to use your own money for your business venture. There are venture capital funds that will give you grants as your base salary to manage the business. All you have to do is present your idea to them, and they will decide if your idea is feasible and good for investment.

If you need more money to grow your business or a team of professionals to help your company go public, applying for venture capital is the right way to go. Those firms provide funds to startups, early-stage, and emerging companies to help them grow and get shares of the startups as compensation, hoping that they will go to IPO or earn significant profits one day. There are many venture capital firms in the market. They provide more than fundings to entrepreneurs at different stages. They may provide guidance and assign advisors to your company to ensure that you are on the right track.

The easiest way to search for such firms is to get the names and contact information from the venture capital associations. You can visit the National Venture Capital Association website for its member list for venture capital firms in the United States.[26] You can visit the Canadian Venture Capital and Private Equity Association member page for the list of Canadian firms.[27] For the United

[26] "NVCA Members", National Venture Capital Association, last accessed September 20, 2023, https://nvca.org/about-us/members/

[27] "Member Directory", Canadian Venture Capital and Private Equity Association, last accessed September 20,

Kingdom, you can visit the British Private Equity & Venture Capital Association's membership page.[28] For other countries, you may have to search for its association first. Of course, not all venture capitals are members of those associations. You will have to search for "venture capital" or "private equity firm" and view individual listings from the search result.

Venture capital firms will look for details about your business before deciding to invest money in it. Specifically, they want to know the following: The Background of the Founders and the Management Team – Do they have appropriate experience and qualifications? The Market Opportunity Size – Is the market size big enough for a successful venture? Your Product – Is it viable and profitable? Market Information – Who are the competitors, and is there any similar product currently available in the market? Your Business Model – How can you make profits from the product? Your Advantages and Benefits – How can your product be differentiated from the others? Intellectual Property – Do you have any, or do you need any patent or copyright? Financial Information – How much are the investments at different stages, with the details of expenses? Return on Investment – What is the projected rate of return,

2023, https://www.cvca.ca/member-resources/member-directory/

[28] "Member Directory", British Private Equity & Venture Capital Association, last accessed September 20, 2023, https://www.bvca.co.uk/Member-Directory

including the possibility of an initial public offering? Legal Challenges – Will there be any legal issues, such as compliances and licenses?

Pitching a venture capital firm is a time-consuming task, so it will be more efficient and time-saving if you can simultaneously approach all the firms and finish your pitching job in a certain period of time. Another downside is that you may have to disclose some confidential information to get the firms' confidence. That may cause a leak of sensitive information, especially when your business model is new and easy to be copied.

A well-drafted business plan can answer all the above questions. Before you approach any venture capital firms, you should have your business plan well drafted. You must tell them how to use the funds to grow your business. When you are given the opportunity to present your idea, your presentation should be concise. If your business involves technical terms, you should use the terminologies that are easily understood by the business people.

Business Plan

Like borrowing money from individuals, you must prepare a business plan for venture capital firms and banks. It helps them understand your business model and management team and increases their confidence in your business. The format of your business plan is much more formal than the one for individuals. Basically, your business plan should include at least the following topics:

Business Overview

You have to describe, in summary, what you are proposing to the venture capital firms. You have to tell your product, your target customers, how you sell, and your growth plans.

Your Edges

You have to address how your product will appeal to customers. How will your product stand out from the crowd, and how will it make a difference in your customers' lives? You should also provide information on competitor weaknesses and strengths and show how you intend to improve on what they are doing.

Market Analysis

You have to do your market research. It helps you understand your customers' needs and how your product can solve their pain points. You should provide information such as your target market size, target customer demographics and geographics, competition, distribution channels, and more.

Organizational Structure

You have to tell the roles and backgrounds of key management team members and the proposed size of your organization. You should also provide information on how you plan to recruit and maintain your employees, including possible outsourced work.

Capital Expenditure

You may need to buy capital goods, such as machinery and technological equipment for your business. The costs of these kinds of capital investments may be relatively high, and the depreciation may be significant. As a result, the assets will be quickly reduced in value, and that causes a higher risk to the investors.

Financial Information

You have to tell how you intend to do with the money and how it will help your business grow. It may involve a few stages, and you have to tell the amount of money you need at each stage, including how the funds will be spent. Venture capital firms only look for companies with the potential for rapid growth or offer an IPO. You may have to project your expenses and revenue with the potential market share projection for a few years.

Government Grants and Subsidies

Governments at all levels and some organizations can provide grants and subsidies to entrepreneurs, especially youth, disabled people, women and indigenous people. However, getting government grants is a challenging task. The competition is keen, and the criteria for awarding the grants are often stringent. For example, you may be disqualified because your residence or business is outside the required geographic location.

Most grants require you to match the grants you are being given, and the amount varies greatly. Different granters may have additional requirements. For example, some granters may require you to find 50% of the total cost by yourself, but they may accept a lower percentage when your venture is research-based.

In addition to a business plan, you will have to submit other information, such as the reasons why you would need the grant. It is like applying for scholarships or bursaries for studying at a university. The criteria are linked with not only the potential but also the needs. Federal and local governments may have different business grants and financing options for small businesses. They may also have special plans on and off, like the COVID-19 emergency plan for business owners and tenants. You can search for the programs available in your country.

Crowdfunding

If you have a good idea and are sure that your product can be produced once enough capital is raised, you may get funding for your venture by raising money through crowdfunding.

Thanks to the Internet, without it, crowdfunding would not have been possible. At least, it cannot be that effective and efficient. There are several crowdfunding sites available, such as IndieGoGo[29] and Kickstarter.[30] All you have to do is to register with them and submit your details. There are two types of crowdfunding – rewards crowdfunding and equity crowdfunding. The supporters (called backers) will contribute their money to support your project by buying your product or shares if they like your idea.

For rewards crowdfunding, entrepreneurs launch their business concept and raise funds by preselling their products at a discount or with special promotional features (collectively called rewards). You set the amount of pledges required for each reward you offer, and the backers select the one they like. One of the benefits is that you may get enough capital to produce the product from invention ideas

[29] "Home page", Indiegogo, last accessed January 7, 2021, https://www.indiegogo.com/
[30] "Home page", Kickstarter, last accessed January 7, 2021, https://www.kickstarter.com/

without incurring debt or sacrificing your company shares, like asking for funds from venture capital firms.

For equity crowdfunding, entrepreneurs launch their business concept and raise funds by offering their company shares to the backers. Such 'public offering' of company shares is only legal in the US, so the sites are all American sites. You should keep the majority of your company shares to remain in control.

In order to succeed in crowdfunding, you should have a prototype or a model of your product ready. You should use videos, pictures and text to present your idea. However, crowdfunding may not be the right place for products that need capital to produce and are easy to copy, as everyone will be able to see your prototype online.

5.   Real Estate

All companies need space to accommodate their business, but they may not have to buy or rent the property. Some people will just start their business at home to avoid paying expensive commercial rent; Microsoft and Apple are typical startups that started their businesses in the garage. However, if you need to acquire real estate space for your business, you will have to know more about your options. It is because, to most companies, real estate is the second-largest expense, just below payroll.

The Need for Real Estate

Unlike human resources, real estate has more options to be acquired, including purchase and lease. Although different options are available, most companies would choose to lease the space to get flexibility and save capital. That is exceptionally true for startups and small firms. Therefore, we will only focus on renting commercial space in this book.

You may think signing a new lease is your only choice for accommodating your business. In fact, there are other options for obtaining space for your business other than that. You can save an office's leasing cost by meeting your clients in the coffee shops or operating your business by sharing space with others (sublease).

You may not need a retail space for your products for retail businesses if you can sell them online or by consignments. Selling by consignments is an excellent way to start your business. Some big corporations also use this approach to sell their high-priced products in department stores, such as cosmetic products. Unfortunately, this approach is outside the scope of this book, and we will not discuss it any further.

Signing a sublease is more or less the same as signing a new lease on your own, except that you may have to deal with two landlords – the head landlord and the sublandlord. You will have to accept the regulations on the lease signed by your sublandlord, which are imposed by the head landlord. The sublandlord may also add other conditions to the sublease. Although allowed in common law, the original lease may have clauses requiring the tenant to get the written consent of the head landlord before subleasing the space.

If you pay the rent to your sublandlord instead of paying the head landlord directly, there is a risk that your sublandlord may just take your money and disappear without paying the head landlord. It may result in the head landlord not receiving the rents, and you have to repay all the rents in arear. In some rare cases, the head landlord may evict you because of the sublandlord's disruption of rent payments.

Before your lease expires, you should analyze if you need to move to another location or not. Usually, you will choose to stay in the same location for several reasons: better negotiation power, better geographic location, the size of the rented space is good, easier to keep your customers, does not incur any moving costs, or simply the landlord is more reliable and reasonable. If this is the case, renewing your lease upon expiry may be a better option than moving to another location. We will talk more about lease renewal in the section below.

When the economy is turning sour, many businesses will consider downsizing by moving to a smaller space, an inferior location, or a building that provides fewer facilities. If you rent space during this period, you should negotiate for a longer lease term with more renewal terms. When you deal with the landlord, you should hire a professional commercial real estate agent to represent you. Otherwise, you may lose money or even worse, you may lose your business for such a mistake.

Types of Space

Commercial real estate leasing is a very complicated task and may involve a significant investment. Therefore, you should treat commercial tenancy seriously from the very beginning before committing to rent any space and should keep a close eye on your lease even after you have moved into the property.

Many people cannot differentiate the differences between commercial tenancies and residential tenancies. Most jurisdictions have different laws to govern the two different types of tenancies. It depends on the nature of your business; you may have to rent a retail space, an industrial property, or just an office unit to accommodate your business needs.

All the leases are quite similar, but each type of lease has special clauses to govern its characteristics. A retail lease will have special clauses to deal with sales, use of space, common area, loading area, parking, trade fixture and operating hours. An industrial lease will have special clauses to deal with environmental issues, indoor and outdoor storage, power supply, and leasehold improvement. An office lease is the simplest among the three types. Still, it will have special provisions to deal with after-office-hour use and parking.

Retail space can be a unit in a shopping mall, a unit in a strip plaza, the ground floor of a live-work building or a stand-alone building. In some cities, retail space can also be at any level of a high-rise building. Some municipalities may also allow some retail space inside an industrial unit or office unit. Of course, the retail unit's exposure and customer traffic are not the same in every case. A better location will have a higher chance of success, but it usually costs a higher price.

Not all retail businesses can be fitted in any retail space. For example, a restaurant will have more restrictions due to its high traffic and fire risk. You have to check the zoning and building requirements for your business in the municipality office before looking for space in that particular municipality. Retail space is the most expensive type, so you may want to minimize your rental space whenever you can. For example, you should fully utilize the retail space by using its height for decorations or storage instead of using the floor area. For restaurants, you should have a reasonable estimate of dine-in, take-out and delivery customers so that you can decide how much dining area you need and will not over rent the space.

Most municipalities will have the most restrictive requirements applied to the location of industrial space due to its pollutive nature. Noise pollution, air pollution, and land and water contamination are all concerns. In order to prevent the pollution from spreading, industrial spaces are often grouped together as industrial parks. Usually, industrial buildings are far apart from residential properties and natural areas. As a result, you have to consider the distance for shipping your goods to your customers. The convenience for your employees going to work is also a factor to be considered.

It is easier to find a warehouse than a site for automobile use. Similarly, it is easier to get a space suitable for garage use than for an automotive body shop because it is difficult to confine airborne paint particles inside the painting room. Although engine oil, gasoline, and other auto-related fluids are also contaminative, they are easier to confine because they are liquid. Again, you have to know your business's requirements, such as zoning requirements, the allowed use of the property, ceiling height, floor loading capacity, power supply, sprinkler system, and more.

Every company needs space for accounting and administrative staff or other office use. Small retailers may use a home office or a portion of their retail space to do the work. Since retail rents are expensive, it is not recommended to use too much retail space for office use. On the other hand, industrial space is an excellent substitute for office space as industrial rents are the lowest among the three types of uses. Many Class C office buildings are, in fact, converted from industrial buildings.

Pick the Right Location

Location, location, location! Although this principle is old, it is always true. Picking the right location may be the key to success in your business venture. It is exceptionally true for a retail location and when the required unit is over tens of thousands of square feet. Sometimes, it takes months, even years, to find a good location. That is why Target was willing to pay over $1.8 billion to buy Zeller's leases when it wanted to expand its operations to Canada in 2011.[31] Otherwise, it would take Target decades, if not impossible, to wait for all the locations to be available one by one.

The success of a retail location relies on the number of customers. First of all, we have to know the Range of your business. A Range is the maximum distance that a consumer would be willing to travel to get that type of product; it can be a driving distance or a walking distance. For example, the Range for coffee shops may be a five-minute drive, but the Range for furniture stores may be an hour's drive. You have to find out the Range of your business type and convert it into a distance. Say a five-minute drive is estimated to be three kilometres equivalent, and a five-minute walk is estimated to be four hundred metres equivalent. Use a map and find out the location of the retail space that you want to rent. Use a compass to set its radius to a scale that is the same as three kilometres (or four hundred metres) on the map. Use the radius to draw a circle on the map using the

---

[31] "Zellers", Wikipedia, last accessed September 20, 2023, https://en.wikipedia.org/wiki/Zellers

retail space's location as the centre. All the people who work or live within the circle are your target customers, by vehicle or on foot.

Not just potential customers, your competitors are also within that circle. Actually, you have to use double the radius to draw another circle. If three centimetres on the map represent the Range of a five-minute drive, you have to use six centimetres as the radius and the same centre to draw another circle on the map. All the competitors who fall into the bigger circle will compete directly with the location you picked.

Once you have the two circles drawn, you can estimate how many potential customers are within the small circle area and how many competitors are within the area of the large circle. Let us use a coffee shop as an example. We have to know that not all people drink coffee, and not every coffee drinker consumes the same number of cups of coffee every day. You have to get those data from a third party, maybe a report from the consulting firms. If 20% of people drink one cup of coffee every day, and there are 20,000 people who work or live within that circle, you will have 4,000 coffee drinkers within your Range. However, not all coffee drinkers are your patrons. You have to know the market share of different coffee shops. Suppose an estimation of only 5% of coffee drinkers would go to your brand (or independent shops). In that case, you will have around 200 customers per day.

However, you also have to know how many competitors there are within the big circle. Those competitors may draw away some of your potential customers, especially those within the small circle. On the other hand, if 200 customers per day are not good enough for your coffee shop to be profitable, you should not consider such a location.

Unlike retail space users, industrial space users spend more money transporting their goods and materials than their rents. Therefore, your factory or warehouse location should be close to your suppliers, customers or shipping ports to save transportation costs and time. The location should also be easy to access by your employees and suppliers. It will be better to have 24-hour transit nearby as your employees may rely on public transportation instead of driving their own cars. The building features are also important, such as ceiling height, power supply, shipping doors, and floor load.

The choice of office space is less complicated than in retail and industrial space. Easy access is the primary concern, so most companies have their office in downtown areas.

Rent Structure

Most rents are charged per square foot or square metre per annum. As a result, it is crucial to know how landlords measure their space. The area used in calculating rent is called the rentable space, which is not the same as the interior space that a tenant can use. The latter one is called the useable space. Landlords charge rent based on the rentable space instead of useable space as that will give them a higher rent. They will tell you how they measure their building size in the lease.

A few sets of measuring methods are used in the market, and the prevailing set is BOMA (Building Owners and Managers Association) standards. BOMA has published different measuring standards in the last few decades, and some of them are still commonly used by landlords. The most controversial one is the 1980 Standard. It would be best to talk to a commercial real estate leasing professional before committing to a lease based on any specific measuring method.

Landlords can charge Gross Rents, Net Rents and Percentage Rents, or a combination of them. Gross rent is the best type for tenants and is also the most straightforward one. The landlord will charge a lump sum of rent that includes property taxes, maintenance, building insurance, and other service charges (such as signage and janitorial services). For office buildings, it is common to include utilities as well.

Net rent is also known as base rent or minimum rent. It is called net rent because it is the net; all other costs will be extra, and it is also the landlord's net profit. All operating expenses paid by the landlord will be transferred to the tenants, known as Additional Rent. Additional rent is all operating costs paid by the landlord and reimbursed by the tenants, but it is called 'rent' for legal reasons. If a landlord charges gross rent, there will be no additional rent chargeable unless it is a hybrid of them. Additional rent is also known as TMI (Taxes, Maintenace and Insurance) for retail plazas, industrial buildings and stand-alone buildings. It is called CAM (Common Area Maintenance) for retail malls, office buildings and structures that have common indoor areas.

Percentage rent is only chargeable on retail space. It is based on an agreed percentage of the tenant's annual gross sales revenue generated from that location. Some low-margin items may be excluded from the sales revenue, such as electronic products and furniture of a department store. A percentage rent can be charged over and above a base rent or a gross rent or in addition to them. When a percentage rent is charged over and above them, the amount payable as the percentage rent will be reduced by the base rent paid. Only the portion above the net rent will be payable. If it is lower than the annual net rent amount, no percentage rent is payable. When a percentage rent is charged in addition to the net rent or gross rent, every dollar in the sales revenue generated at that location will be subject to the percentage rent.

A percentage rent can be used as the only rent charged without any gross or net rent. That is, the rent is independent of the size of the space you rented. A lease based on pure percentage rent is usually for a small space, such as a kiosk or a fast-food restaurant in the food court or a particular section inside a department store. That is the best rent structure for retail tenants, as the rent is a percentage of their sales revenue, which is a variable cost. The tenant only has to pay a high rent amount if its sales revenue is high. Of course, it is not easy to negotiate for a pure percentage rent lease.

Lease Term

You should sign a lease to protect your rights. A commercial lease term is typically five years long, but it can be shorter or longer. Since a lease is a contract of commitment, the more years in the lease term, the longer you are committed to renting the place. Thus, you may not have the flexibility to move to another location within that lease term for any reason. However, some tenants, such as the government, may be able to negotiate for a break-up clause to end the lease upon giving the landlord a six-month or nine-month notice.

In most jurisdictions, there is no requirement for the landlord or the tenant to notify the other party to terminate the tenancy when the lease term expires. Once a commercial lease term ends, the tenant must move out unless the landlord is willing to let the tenant stay behind. On the other hand, most commercial tenancies laws allow the landlord to increase the rent to double the amount of the current rent if the tenant stays without the landlord's consent after the lease expires.

Having a long lease term can secure the tenant's right to stay on the premises for a long period, but it increases the commitment and liabilities in case the tenant wants to move or terminate the lease. Instead of committing to a long lease term, it is better to negotiate for the right to renew your lease for additional terms.

An option to renew a lease is a common practice in commercial real estate leasing. It gives the tenants the right to renew their lease if they want. On the other hand, the tenant does not have to stay on the premises if they decide not to renew the lease. Such a right gives the tenants flexibility, so most tenants will ask for it when negotiating the lease terms with the landlord.

An option to renew can be for one additional term or more. Everything in a lease will be renewed the same as the initial lease terms except for the rent. The renewal terms' length usually will be the same as the initial term, but they do not have to. Say you sign a lease term for five years; your renewal term can be three years or seven years. Of course, the same term length (five years in this case) is the most common arrangement. How many times can a tenant renew its lease? It can be one, but it can be five or more. It is an issue that must be negotiated before the first lease is signed. The tenants would try to get as many times to renew as they can since it is free and beneficial to them. On the opposite, the landlords would try to limit the number of times the tenants can renew the lease.

In most cases, the landlords will put a clause in the leases to stipulate that the new rents for renewed terms will be based on the market rents at the renewal time. Some big tenants, however, are able to negotiate a pre-agreed rent for their renewals. Since it is challenging to project market rents for a few decades, those big tenants usually can get much more favourable rents. One example is Sears; when it closed its operations in Canada, Sears sold five of its leases back to the landlords and earned $400 million because of its extra-low pre-agreed rents.[32]

---

[32] "Sears Canada sells Toronto flagship store and 4 others, putting hundreds out of work", Financial Post, last updated October 29, 2013,

To conclude, you should hire a competent commercial real estate agent in the field you need – retail, industrial, office or else. The agent should be able to protect you and introduce more options to you.

_____

https://financialpost.com/news/retail-marketing/sears-canada-abandons-toronto-flagship-store-and-4-others-putting-hundreds-out-of-work

6. Marketing and Sales

Marketing is a rich and important subject, and it may take several courses to explain it fully. The few issues to be discussed here are the basic concepts an entrepreneur must understand, but other marketing techniques may also interest you.

What is marketing? According to the American Marketing Association,

> *Marketing is the activity, set of institutions, and processes for creating, communicating, delivering, and exchanging offerings that have value for customers, clients, partners, and society at large.*[33]

A more direct and practical definition was given by The New York Times,

> *Marketing is the art of telling stories so enthralling that people lose track of their wallets.*[34]

---

[33] "Definitions of Marketing", American Marketing Association, last accessed September 20, 2023, https://www.ama.org/the-definition-of-marketing-what-is-marketing/

[34] "Why Don't You Donate for Syrian Refugees? Blame Bad Marketing", The New York Times, last updated June 14,

It does not matter how good your product is; it has no sales if it cannot reach the customers. That is why marketing is so important. The most crucial concept in marketing is the Marketing Mix. Marketing Mix is a term that sets the foundation model for businesses. Historically, it consists of four basic terms – Product, Price, Place, and Promotion, also known as the "4 Ps".

Product

We talked about a product a little bit in Chapter Two. A product is a tangible or intangible object made available for consumer use. Tangible products can be foods, drinks, and pens. Intangible products include all kinds of services and nonphysical goods such as trademarks and other intellectual properties.

Your product has to stand out from its competitors; product differentiation is one of the strategies to achieve such a goal. That is, how can your product be different from similar products currently available in the market? If your product is a cellphone, it may have a better camera, a faster Internet speed, a lighter body, a more powerful battery, a shorter recharge time, or just a better look.

2017,
https://www.nytimes.com/2017/06/14/business/medi
a/marketing-charity-water-syria.html

On the other hand, we can market the same product from different aspects. A pen with an 18K gold body and small diamonds is, of course, a luxury writing instrument. However, it can also be marketed as a piece of jewellery, and such positioning may differentiate it better and more efficiently.

A story shared by one of my students is more interesting. He was a commercial real estate broker. One day, a client approached him, saying that the government would expropriate her land, and she asked for a better solution. The land was about five acres and zoned for automotive use. It was rented to a tenant, who used it as a junk site for dumping used vehicles. Therefore, the government offered her the price of a junk site instead of a regular commercial site. Although the expropriation eased her concern about possible contamination caused by the used vehicles, the owner wanted to negotiate for a better price, so she asked my student for help.

Since the site was zoned for automotive use, my student considered changing its image from a junk site to a future auto-dealership site. He sent out request-for-proposal to all automobile manufacturers, including motorcycle makers. Three of them replied with interest, and the prices they offered were 10 to 20 times the price the government used for expropriation. Eventually, he negotiated for a price that was around 11 times the original compensation in the expropriation. In this case, the product was the land, and its use did not change during the process.

My student changed the image of the site from a junk site to a new car dealership site to increase its price. It is similar to branding, packaging and labelling – all can increase the value of a product without changing the product itself.

Price

Price is the amount of money that a product asks, or customers pay for a product in the market. Setting your prices is one of the crucial steps in setting up your business model. It is determined by several factors, including market share, competition, material costs, product identity and the customer's perceived value of the product.

Pricing is strongly linked with your market positioning. Marketing positioning refers to the position that a product occupies in the customers' minds and how it is distinguished from the competitors. Simply speaking, a pen with an 18K gold body is at the luxury products level, while a disposable pen is at the low-end market level. The positioning actually has multi-dimensions; price, quality, functions, and brand are just a few of them. For the same product, setting a different price may have a different impact on it.

There are five basic pricing strategies:

Competitive pricing:	Set the price based on what the competitors charge.
Cost-plus pricing:	Add a mark-up to the total costs of the product.
Penetration pricing:	Set a low price to enter a competitive market and raise it later.
Price skimming:	Set a high price and lower it as the market evolves.
Value-based pricing:	Set a price based on how much the customer believes the product is worth.

Below is a true story to show how a low pricing strategy can, sometimes, adversely affect the sales of a product.

A teenager asked his wealthy dad to give him one thousand dollars to buy a nice jacket in a department store. The dad struggled a little bit but handed the teenager one thousand dollars to buy the jacket. When the dad asked his son to show him the jacket the next day, his son handed back the money and said, "I didn't buy it."

"Why?" the dad curiously asked.

"When I went to the department store this morning, I found that the jacket was on sale. It is now selling for $300 only. I don't want my friends to know that I would buy a jacket that is sold for that cheap."

That is why some designer brands will never offer significant discounts, clearance sales, or operate factory outlets.

Another pricing story is about Target Canada. It spent over $1.8 billion to buy all the lease agreements of Zellers stores in Canada.[35] In a shocking move, it exited the Canadian market after losing more than $5 billion in just two years.[36] As a consumer, I found that its prices were much higher than those of its rival – Walmart. Even when it decided to close all its stores and offered clearance sales, most of its products were still more expensive than those in Walmart. I would say a wrong pricing strategy is the main cause of its failure.

---

[35] "Target Canada", Wikipedia, last accessed September 20, 2023, https://en.wikipedia.org/wiki/Target_Canada

[36] "In surprise move, Target exits Canada and takes $5.4 billion loss", Reuters, last updated January 15, 2015, https://www.reuters.com/article/us-target-canada-idUSKBN0KO1HR20150115

Place

A place is a process of making a product available for the customers who need it. That is, a place represents the location where a product can be purchased or the channel where the product can go through to be placed for sale. Therefore, a place is often referred to as the distribution channel.

A distribution channel may include any physical stores as well as virtual stores on the Internet. For online stores, a distribution channel may refer to the media, the network, and how your message is delivered, and your online store is linked. You may have an excellent product, but you cannot succeed without having the right distribution channel to deliver it.

There are three types of distributions:

Intensive Distribution (also known as Mass Distribution): You set up as many channels as possible. The goal of the intensive distribution is to penetrate as much of the market as possible. Most consumer goods use this kind of distribution.

Selective Distribution: You select the channels in specific locations or nature. It is often used for specialty products, restricting the number of outlets handling the products so that the manufacturers can target a particular market of consumers. It usually caps the number of channels in a specific area.

Exclusive Distribution: You make your products available only in particular locations or stores so that you retain greater control over the distribution process. Luxury products use this method to maintain the brand's image and product exclusivity.

It may be a good idea for you to have the big chain stores sell your products as their order quantity is much higher than independent ones. Serving one big chain store may be easier than serving thousands of independent ones. In most cases, it also makes the logistics much easier for you as you have to ship to their distribution centre only instead of sending to individual independent stores.

However, big chain stores often ask for a credit period of not less than 90 days. It means that you will have to supply four months' supplies to them before getting one month's payment. Moreover, if your products are fast-moving consumer goods, they would also ask for free trial samples in each store. That can be thousands of pieces, and your costs can be quite significant.

If your business is an online store or a website for people to use your service, you need high traffic to your website. How to increase the traffic is the key to success.

There are many ways to do that. If you have a budget for advertising, you may try advertising on search engines, social media, or other websites. You may also hire professionals for Search Engine Optimization (SEO), which targets unpaid traffic and usually is a one-time expense.

If you do not have a budget for advertising or hiring professionals for SEO, you may use social media channels to promote your site. You may also do the SEO yourself. The first step you should take is to choose a good domain name (website name) for your business. There are two ways to select your domain name – your brand name or your business type. For brand names, examples include google.com, amazon.com, and apple.com. For business types, examples are hotels.com and tripadvisor.com.

Having a website in your company or product name is the right way to go, as it gives a positive image to the customers and protects the brand name by preventing other people from using it. However, it may not be a good idea in SEO, especially when you do not advertise your website. For example, if you are a realtor and your name is Leslie Doe, you may want to register the domain name lesliedoe.com. You wish the home buyers and sellers to visit your website and eventually hire you as their agent. They will not know Leslie Doe and hire you as their agent unless they search the Internet and find your website.

The problem is that if they do not know you, they will not search for Leslie Doe, and your website will not come out on the first few pages of the result. If they know you, they probably know your website address and do not need to search for it. They may also have your business card. In either case, those people are your friends or acquaintances, so they are not the online target visitors. People who do not know you will not see your website on the search engines, as they will not search for your name. For people who know you, they do not need to search for your website.

Instead of using your name, Leslie Doe, you may consider using keywords that people will use when searching for homes or realtors. The domains with the words real estate, homes, houses, and for sale will have better SEO than those based on your name. For example, if you want to trade real estate in Any City, you may consider the domain name anycityhomes.com, anycitycondosforsale.com, or luxuryhomesanycity.com. Of course, if you are trading in a big town or city, most of the domains may have been taken. You may try using variations such as anycityhomeforsale (without 's'), anycity-homesforsale, or any-city-homes-for-sale.

Having a good domain name will give you a leap in your business venture.

Promotion

Promotion is all the communications that a marketer may use to inform target audiences of a product; most of the time, it is persuasive in nature. A promotion should be formulated to reach an attainable goal, be presented in a unique way that engages its audience and should showcase your product throughout its course.

Promotion has four distinct elements: advertising, public relations, personal selling and sales promotion. Advertising can be carried out in physical environments, such as at events such as concerts and trade shows. They can be done via traditional media such as magazines and newspapers, electronic media such as radio and television, and outdoor media such as banners or billboard signs. They can also be made via digital media, including Internet search results, social media sites, video games and cellphone apps. Public relations are usually done by sponsoring social events, such as sports or charities. Personal selling may cost the most resources but may also be the most effective promotional method. Sales promotion can be done by combining all the above means, including promotional kiosks in a shopping mall.

Not all products will fit in the same promotion. A designer brand will never use radio commercials to promote its brand image, while a politician will not use fashion magazines to promote their schemes.

You may consider creating a slogan for your business. Usually, a slogan is for a brand rather than a single product. It captures the ideology, mission, personality and values in a few words. Since it may be the first impression a business makes on consumers and projects a vital component of a brand's image, a slogan must be carefully worded. There are well-known slogans such as *"Just Do It"* by Nike,[37] *"Think Different"* by Apple[38] and *"A Diamond is Forever"* by De Beers.[39] I created a slogan for my company, *"We Are Small, But We Are Professional!"*.[40]

Many corporations and individuals distribute free items to customers or the public to promote their businesses or products. The most common things are calendars, pens, mugs, memo pads and sticky notes. We cannot say which one is the best for your business, but there are some items that you should avoid.

One of the old-fashioned types of promotional items is keychains. It was a 'necessity' in the old days when people had just one key or two because they needed the keychain to

---

[37] "Just Do It", Wikipedia, last accessed September 20, 2023, https://en.wikipedia.org/wiki/Just_Do_It

[38] "Think different", Wikipedia, last accessed September 20, 2023, https://en.wikipedia.org/wiki/Think_different

[39] "De Beers", Wikipedia, last accessed September 20, 2023, https://en.wikipedia.org/wiki/De_Beers

[40] "Home page", Prodigy Consulting, last accessed September 20, 2023, http://www.prodigy.ca/

hold the little keys. Now, the keys are bigger in size for better security, including the car keys with remote control and RFID functions. Keychains become a burden. Moreover, even if people need keychains, who will carry a bulky (and usually ugly) keychain with words on its surface just to advertise for you?

Magnets and magnetic business cards are also common promotional items. Their function is to hold some notes on a metal surface so that people will put them on the fridge and see your information on them every day. The problem is that most of those magnets are not strong enough to hold even a piece of small note but just themselves. Unlike the souvenir magnets we buy in tourist areas, promotional magnets are not good decorators. No one will use them if they cannot hold any paper. It is like a keychain that cannot hold any key.

Another ineffective promotional item you should not waste money on is a bag of seeds. Unlike the keychain and magnet, many people welcome such a freebie, especially those with a front yard or backyard. Once, I received a bag of flower seeds from the realtors trading in our neighbourhood. I liked those seeds and could not wait to plant them in my front yard, and they grew well. All my visitors loved the flowers and asked me where to buy the seeds. My answer was that they were a promotional item from a realtor whose name is …? Who will keep the package with the information of the realtor once the seeds are planted? That realtor should have saved the money in the flower seeds and used the money somewhere else.

A newer promotional item is a USB drive, and it is an expensive item, too. While almost all promotional items cost less than a dollar, this type of hi-tech gadget costs at least a few dollars each. The problem is that such a hi-tech product can easily become obsolete. The memory size of the first free USB drive I got from the promoter was only 8 Megabytes. The next one was 32 Megabytes, but both of them are now in the dumpsite. Expensive or hi-tech items are not suitable for free promotional use.

You have to consider not only the cost of promotional items but also the usage of them. If people do not keep it or use it, it is not a good idea at all.

Payment

I suggested that Payment be included in the marketing mix and have been the advocate since 2008. Payment is vital as ease and security of transactions play crucial roles in marketing, especially in the cyber age. If you are in the retail field, you should provide easy and secure payment methods to your customers for a better shopper experience.

Payment is the consideration for the delivery of goods and services. Traditionally, retailers would try to provide as many payment options as possible for the convenience of their customers and hence attract more business. Cash, debit cards, cheques, gift vouchers, and different types of credit cards (such as VISA, Master, American Express, Diners Club, JBC and Discovery) are commonly accepted in most establishments, especially the big department stores. It is inconvenient for customers to bring a large amount of cash to dine in luxury restaurants or buy luxury products in shopping malls. Alternative payment methods are crucial for retailers as well as other businesses.

Many merchants offer bonus points to their customers, such as mileage points offered by airline companies, club points provided by retail stores and airtime points offered by mobile phone companies. Some loyalty programs are provided by third parties, too. Those are incentives to the customers, but all those points are also a kind of payment itself. Customers can redeem the points for products or directly apply them to pay for the purchased goods and services.

In the cyber age, easy and secure payment methods are essential for all online transactions. Can you imagine an online store that will accept only cash or ask its customers to send in a bank draft to buy their products? Payment is not just a tool in marketing; it is one of the necessities.

Many payment methods use RFID (radio-frequency identification) technology for faster and more secure payment methods. Mastercard's PayPass, VISA's PayWave, the Octopus card in Hong Kong and the Oyster Card in the UK are a few good examples. Cellphone manufacturers have launched the idea of digital wallets – using your cell phone to make payments and as proof of ID. The 'smartphone-enabled wallet' allows consumers to purchase items simply by tapping their phone on a pad at the cashier, much like a tap-and-pay credit card, but it can also have GPS and ID to serve other purposes.

Actually, all companies that deal with payments, such as credit cards, PayPal, Alipay and Apple Pay, are payment processing companies that ensure the payees and the payors have secured and easy transactions. They make profits by charging the merchants a commission, usually a percentage of the sales. Sometimes, they will also charge a flat fee or a monthly fee in addition to the commission rate. Some may also charge the payors when people pay their credit card fees using non-credit card payment services.

Suppose your business needs to accept online or retail payments. In that case, you should spend some time studying the differences among different payment processing companies, including their security level, commission rate, flat fee, monthly fee, transaction fee, payment time and chargeback policy.

Other Marketing Issues

Packaging

Marketing people have always emphasized the importance of packaging. It is the way to make a first impression on the customers. It is crucial to make the customers feel that the product is valuable by using high-quality packaging, especially for the products that people would buy as presents. However, some people believe packaging should be a part of a product, and some people think it is a part of a promotion.

Because of the advanced packaging technology today, products are now protected from contamination, crushing, breakage, and spoilage, and it helps the product be unaffected by climatic conditions. Packaging can also be used in elaborating necessary details about the product, company, quantity, ingredients, precautions, expiry date, and more.

In some extreme cases, such as some fancy chocolate items, the cost of packaging may exceed the cost of the product itself to attract customers. Actually, the images of singers, actors, actresses, and even politicians are based on packaging. They are just what they projected in your mind. How to package an actor or actress is vital to make a movie star. How to package a politician is crucial to get the trust of the public.

People

All people involved in the operation of a business are important, including workers, salesforce, management, and more. People are important assets in service industries such as travel agencies, restaurants, hair salons and entertainment businesses. No two persons are the same, and no two persons can provide the same service to customers, or the effect will not be the same. The best example is using different actors and actresses to play the characters in a movie. Therefore, it is crucial to recruit good people and maintain good quality service to attract and keep customers.

It is common to see advertisements saying that "All our technicians are certified", "our service consultants are all well trained and licensed", "all our instructors have over ten years of experience in the field", and so on. However, such guarantees can only warrant that their people have achieved a certain level of education or experience. There is no assurance that their service will be great. To standardize the effect and to minimize the gap among different people, the term Process is introduced.

Process

A process is a procedure, mechanism and flow of activities to provide service or produce a product. The prevailing ISO standards (such as ISO 9001) are designed to help organizations ensure their process can meet customers' and other stakeholders' needs in their field. A well-organized and quality-controlled process may reduce the difference in quality performed by different people.

Using a checklist is a simple step to ensure the process is well done. Many auto shops offer free courtesy checks on your vehicle when they change engine oil for you. New car dealerships will also check your cars for defeats during the warranty period to ensure high-quality services. Such checking cannot rely on the technicians' experience; a checklist is the best tool for doing such a job. A typical process that many homemakers use every day is a recipe. Instead of relying on the chef's memory and experience, a recipe records the ingredients as well as the method of cooking. A process is a crucial tool used in human resources training, too.

Physical Evidence

Physical Evidence may refer to tangible and intangible elements. It allows the consumers to make judgments about that organization. It includes some of the following: premises, websites, paperwork (such as air tickets), brochures, signage (such as those on aircraft and vehicles), uniforms, and business cards.

Just imagine that if you bought a ticket for the 2016 Olympic Games online, you would love to show your friends the 'official ticket' and keep it as a souvenir instead of printing a bar code from your computer. A traditionally printed ticket with a hologram will serve the purpose. That is one of the examples of Physical Evidence.

Scent Marketing

Most people will not buy a perfume without knowing its fragrance. Not just for perfumes, scents may attract people and increase their desire to buy your products. Some retail merchants may subtly diffuse pleasant aromas to attract customers, hence increasing their willingness to buy. Scenting allows the stores to connect with consumers on an emotional level and make the establishment more powerful and memorable. Such a strategy is best used in establishments such as coffee shops and bakeries.

Basic Selling Techniques

A business cannot survive with no sales. A competent salesforce is crucial to the success of a business. That is why most companies offer attractive commission packages in addition to base salaries to their salespeople as the incentive for higher sales volume.

You have to know the advantages of your product, but it is more important to know the benefits that your product can bring to your customers. For example, you are a pen manufacturer and are selling disposable pens at a low price. Disposable and low prices are the advantages, but they may not be the benefits to your customers. Say your target customers are wealthy people, so they do not mind paying a higher price to keep the pen for life. An expensive pen can show off their wealthy status; hence, the advantages of your disposable pen cannot bring any benefit to those customers. On the other hand, they may bring benefits to those customers who are budget-conscious.

Therefore, a good salesperson knows how to probe to find out the customers' needs and provide a "solution". If they need a luxury pen, you may point out that a luxury pen may not be suitable for everyday use or for other people to use it. Buying a disposable pen is an excellent auxiliary to a luxury pen. Of course, not every time a salesperson will succeed. That is why many people said salespersons are "paid to be rejected". They will be rejected many times until they make a sale.

Consequently, salespersons must be hardworking as the chance of a successful sale is not high, so they have to keep calling and be prepared to be rejected. Many successful salespersons are not born to be selling machines, and they did not receive proper salesmanship training either. They learnt selling skills by practicing. They had been repeatedly rejected before they could make a successful sale. Consistent effort is a must for all successful salespeople.

We have to work hard and work smart. Therefore, successful salespeople must be smart enough to provide customers with different options to resolve their objections or problems. Such options are usually linked with your pricing model or product line. A salesperson may offer a quantity discount to a customer, provide installments for high-priced products, or offer different products with different features to solve a customer's problem. That is quite common in selling computer hardware such as desktop computers, printers and monitors.

A good salesperson also has to have a positive mindset. The popular story below demonstrates how a good salesperson thinks:

Two salespersons of a shoe factory were sent to a small country in Africa to explore business opportunities about 100 years ago. When they came back, the boss interviewed them one by one.

The first salesman said: "Don't waste your time, boss. All the people there do not wear shoes. There is no market for us."

The second salesman said: "No one sells shoes there. We can have millions of shoes sold, and I think we should hire more people to operate our production lines 24/7."

Therefore, it is crucial to hire salespersons with a positive attitude, creative thinking and assertive personality. However, it is also vital to ensure that they will be ethical and treat customers with honesty and integrity. Having a good sales team can give you a big step towards success.

7. Governing Laws

We are all supposed to be law-abiding citizens, and all legitimate businesses are supposed to trade legally. Although most of us and most companies are, many companies unintentionally or deliberately violate the laws. Although some of them luckily avoided their liabilities, most of those companies have closed or fined heavily because of that. You have to be cautious about the laws in your country, state or province, and municipality.

Licenses and Permits

As you may have known from the stories of Microsoft and Apple, many startups started their business in their founders' garage. That is a home business setup. A home business is allowed in most municipalities with different conditions. In general, you can only use a certain percentage of your home for business use, and the norm is 25%. However, certain businesses are prohibited in most municipalities, such as manufacturing, medical-related or food-related. You may not be allowed to put any signage, and parking may also be an issue. You should inform your insurance company to ensure that your home insurance coverage will not be voided because of your home business. Depending on your business nature, there may be an increase in the premium.

If you have to rent a retail or industrial unit for your business, you should talk to a competent commercial real estate broker, as there are zoning bylaws that affect the use of your unit. Two buildings with the same zoning code may have different uses due to the parking bylaws. The one with a bigger site has ample parking space so that it can be a dine-in restaurant. The one with a smaller site may not have enough parking spaces, so it can only be a take-out and delivery restaurant. Sometimes, you want to have the flexibility to do it. For example, an industrial-zoned unit with a percentage of retail use allowed may be a good place for manufacturing, showroom and retail use.

Some businesses may require obtaining a permit from the municipal or regional government, such as restaurants. Some may require licenses from other authorities, such as liquor-related or transportation-related businesses.

Employment

When you have to hire people to work for you, you should know some basic requirements of employment-related laws such as the income tax law, human rights law and labour law in your country. Although the laws in different countries are not the same, they have a similar nature.

Hiring a person to work for you as an independent contractor is an alternate method for hiring that person as an employee. It saves you some employment costs such as payroll admin costs, pension plans and employment insurance contributions. Since the company does not have to make tax deductions from independent contractors' earnings, they will have more before tax available to them. Moreover, independent contractors have more flexible work terms than employees. Therefore, it may be a win-win arrangement for both 'employers' and 'employees'.

When advertising for your employment requirements, you should be sensitive not to use any phrases that are discriminative under the human rights law. For example, you may want to explore the China market and want to hire a salesperson for that purpose. It would be best not to use phrases like "… Chinese salesperson wanted". Instead, you should say, "… speaks Mandarin and has connections with China". Similarly, we should use the word "energetic" instead of "young" to avoid ageism.

Some jurisdictions also do not allow discrimination against people other than common human rights grounds. For example, an employer cannot require a minimum body height, maximum weight, or criminal records (with or without pardon) unless those requirements are bona fide occupational qualifications (known as BFOR), such as no criminal record for police officers.

Many jurisdictions have laws to govern occupational health and safety. Employers are required to provide training and protective equipment for the protection of their employees. For example, an employer may have to provide masks and gloves to the employees when working in a dusty environment.

Privacy

Sending emails may be the most excellent way to promote a business, especially for B2C companies. Emailing is a fast method to reach potential customers. It can redirect the readers to the company's website and contain videos and photos; those functions are not available in printed materials. Most importantly, it is free of charge. However, sending emails to people without their explicit consent may have violated the privacy law.

Many countries have privacy laws that prohibit companies and individuals from sending unsolicited emails to people without their consent. Senders cannot send emails to them and ask them to opt out if they do not want to receive your email anymore. That is, recipients must opt-in to receive the emails.

Similar laws may also exist to prohibit cold callings by phone. The authority may have a Do Not Call List for people to register if they do not want to receive any sales calls. Once a number is registered on that list, a telemarketer cannot call that number.

Many businesses are also involved in collecting personal data from their customers, such as photo ID for complying with money laundry laws, credit card number for the transaction, name, telephone number and address for delivery. Companies are required to store that information securely, use it only for related services and destroy it once the information is no longer required.

Copyright and Patent

If you develop a new product with new technology or design, you may want to protect your intellectual property with a patent. Similarly, you can also protect your business name, slogans, and logos by registering a trademark.

Not all kinds of design or technology can be patented, and a patent is only valid in the country where it is granted. Therefore, you may have to file an international application to the World Intellectual Property Organization (WIPO) in your country. Under the Patent Cooperation Treaty, your patent application will be filed in as many as 153 member countries through a single international application. However, The granting of patents remains the authority of each national patent office. That is, you may have to get them registered one by one. A patent agent should be hired for such a task.

A trademark can be your brand name, your logo, or a slogan. It is crucial for a business to have a brand and a logo that are distinctive from the others. Similar to the registration of a patent, a trademark is registered locally in a country, and you will have to register it in other countries one by one.

Taxes

Tax laws are complicated, and different laws apply to businesses in different ways. Some of them give business owners rights to claim tax benefits, and some of them require owners to fulfill their obligations. Most businesses are required to collect sales taxes for the government. When collecting the sales tax, all companies act as agents for the government. They pay sales tax to their suppliers, and they charge sales tax from their customers at the same time. They have to submit the difference after deducting the sales tax they paid from the amount they collected. They can deduct the sales tax paid to the suppliers from the sales tax collected from their customers. However, if they pay more than they charge, they can ask the government to pay them back the difference. Eventually, their sales tax account balance will be zero after filing the tax to the government.

Some jurisdictions make the registration of sales tax accounts voluntary if the sales volume of the business does not exceed a certain amount. However, since the company can claim back the sales tax paid to the suppliers, it is a better option for a business to register regardless of how much sales volume it can generate.

As an entrepreneur, you should have some basic understanding of tax sheltering methods available to your business. Individuals trade as sole proprietors or partnerships, and corporations are permitted to have tax allowances for the expenses they pay. The first type of tax allowance is depreciation for equipment and assets purchased. It is called Capital Cost Allowance (CCA) in Canada and called Capital Allowance in the UK.

Since capital assets are usually large purchases, most governments will allow business owners to claim depreciation of their equipment. The government acknowledges the existence of depreciation that is the result of wear and tear over the life of a capital asset and the ability to offset income to the cost of that asset.

Most of the depreciation calculations will be spread over a few years, with some exceptions that may be done in one year (such as glassware or chinaware) or over decades (such as real estate). The depreciation amount claimed in that year can be deducted from the taxable business income of the same year, hence reducing the tax payable.

Strictly speaking, depreciation is not a tax-saving tool but a tax-deferring tool. It is because you may have to pay back the tax you saved by claiming depreciation after the sale of the equipment if the actual depreciation is less than the amount you have claimed. Since real estate will appreciate over a long period of time, it is likely that you may have to repay the tax reduced by the depreciation when you sell the real property.

Different classes of equipment have different depreciation rates that the taxpayer can claim for their depreciation. For example, most real properties in Canada are under Class One with a depreciation rate of 4%. In the United States, real estate has a depreciation rate of 3.636%, but it is less than 1% in the United Kingdom. A building may collapse or need to be demolished, but the land will last forever. Therefore, only the values of the building and other improvements are depreciable; the land value is not.

Most tax laws do not apportion the depreciation for the year the equipment is purchased. That is, the depreciation will be the same regardless of whether the purchase is made at the beginning of the year or the end of it. That is why most corporations will buy their equipment before their fiscal year-end to maximize the use of depreciation. When you buy a piece of equipment on Jan 1, you may claim the depreciation of that year, but you can claim depreciation for one more year if you buy it one day before, on Dec 31 of the previous year.

There may be other tax benefits that a startup may enjoy. It would be helpful if you talk to an accountant or tax lawyer for more information.

8.   Franchise

Most franchisors are successful business people and experts in the field of their business. They know their business inside and out. Due to their success, they decided to franchise their business and start teaching other people (the franchisees) how to utilize their business model to make profits. In addition to the know-how, franchisors also provide equipment, training, and products to franchisees, as well as the right to use their intellectual property, such as logos and slogans. Some of them even provide financing to their franchisees.

Buying a Franchise as a Venture

In Chapter 1, we have talked about the definition of an entrepreneur. According to the Merriam-Webster dictionary and Oxford dictionary, an entrepreneur is basically the one *who organizes, manages, and assumes the risks of a business.* Simply speaking, an entrepreneur is a business owner who also manages the business personally. Therefore, owning a franchise business also fits into the idea of entrepreneurship.

All franchisors are supposed to be proven successful business owners with track records. Because of its well-established business model and reputation, a franchise business usually has a higher success rate than an independent business. Moreover, since franchisors will provide training to the franchisees, it is easier for a person without adequate business knowledge and experience to run a business from scratch. However, not all franchisors are good, and not all franchisees will succeed even if the franchisor is good.

Some people said buying a franchise is like paying money to get hired to work. That is an unfair comment, as purchasing a franchise allows you to learn how the franchisor, a successful business operator, runs a business. From there, you may learn something that the school will not teach you or takes a long time to understand without practicing. Moreover, the franchise business may bring you a considerable financial reward that is incomparable to any job. Therefore, selecting a reputable franchise business with the potential to grow is of utmost importance.

First of all, you should talk to the existing franchisees if possible. They know the quality and value of the franchise business and the reputation of the franchisor. That is from the point of view of a franchisee, but not as a consumer. Some franchise businesses have an outstanding reputation among consumers, but only the insiders know they are harsh on their franchisees.

Beware of Internal Competition

From one store to a chain of stores, from a chain of stores to a franchise business, most franchisors would sell their stores to the franchisees and keep only one store in each state or province as a role model and training facility. However, some franchisors may keep tens or over one hundred stores. Some even have hundreds of corporate stores worldwide. Since there is no difference between the corporate-owned and franchisees' stores in the consumers' eyes, as their names and logos are the same, those corporate-owned stores are directly competing with their franchisees.

All franchisees have to pay a franchise fee to run the franchise business for a limited period, usually seven to ten years. Once the franchise period expires, the franchisees will have to renew the franchise agreement by paying a franchise fee again. Most franchisors will sign the leases with the landlord directly and sublet the space to their franchisees for retail franchise businesses. As a result, a franchisee cannot stay on the same premises if the franchise agreement is not renewed for any reason.

Most franchisors reserve their right to relocate the renewed franchisee to another location. It happened to one international franchise business. Their most profitable franchisee had to renew the franchise agreement, and the franchisor relocated that franchisee to another location. The reason for the relocation was that the franchisor wanted the outlet with top performance to be its corporate-owned store so that the franchisor could make more profit.

To protect yourself, you should check how many corporate-owned outlets a franchisor owns before buying its franchise. If the franchisor is a member of a local franchise association, you may get that information from the website of that association. If not, you can ask that franchisor directly; they should have the information for you. Keep in mind that it is common for a franchisor to have corporate-owned stores; it only becomes suspicious when they have too many.

The Location and Lease

Well-established franchisors have very limited choices for new franchisees to select their locations. They often want new franchisees to explore new markets in small towns, remote areas, or overseas. You may have to relocate in order to get the franchise. It would be best to do your own research on the location, including using the Range discussed in Chapter 5 to estimate the sales revenue generated at that location.

As mentioned in the above section, most franchisors signed the lease with the landlords and sublet the premises to the franchisee. The purpose is to control the leasehold ownership so that a franchisee cannot stay behind as an independent operator once the franchise agreement is terminated or expired.

On the other hand, some franchisors will ask their franchisees to sign the leases with the landlords without getting the franchisors involved. Their reason is that they do not want to spend resources on administrating the leases. Most franchisors will not do that as they will lose control of the premises. In case the location is an excellent one for their business type, the franchisee can opt not to renew the franchise agreement and become an independent merchant at the same place.

One franchisor asked its franchisees to sign their lease with the landlords directly when it wanted to expand its operation rapidly. It opened over 100 stores within 12 months, but most of those new stores closed within one year due to over-expansion. That might be why the franchisor did not want to be involved in the lease – to avoid liability when the franchisees failed. You should pay extra caution when a franchisor refuses to be involved in leasing the premises where a franchisee operates the business.

Moreover, many franchisors often overrent space for their franchisees. Again, it would help if you use the Range to estimate how many customers you will have to serve each day to project the space you need. Using the Percentage Rent as an alternative rental payment is an excellent way to avoid high basic rent.

Unfair Practice

Some franchisors fail to think in the best interests of franchisees; instead, they conduct unfair practices and are not attentive to the franchisees' P & L statements. Such a franchise will not be successful; at least, it will not bring big profits to its franchisees as other successful franchisors do. They often have unfair terms and conditions in their franchise agreements to give them such rights, so you must carefully read the agreement with the assistance of a professional before signing it.

It is a norm to require all franchisees to buy their merchandise from the franchisor to unify their product lines. Moreover, centralizing the merchandising department can give the franchisor a more substantial bargaining power, and all franchisees may benefit from the bargained wholesale price. However, not all franchisors would transfer those benefits to their franchisees.

One popular fast-food franchise got wholesale prices from its suppliers, but it charged its franchisees higher than the retail prices. For example, the regular price of a can of cola was only 25 cents at the supermarkets. The franchisor charged its franchisees 30 cents each. Although the franchisees could still make a profit as their price at the fast-food outlet was $1.00 each, the franchisees had to pay a price much higher than the sale price that supermarkets offered, which could be less than 20 cents each.

Another franchisor required all its franchisees to buy products from it and offered a 40% discount on its retail prices. However, such a discount rate was fixed regardless of any promotion that the franchisor held nationwide. For example, some products were advertised for a 70% discount during the Boxing Week Sale, and the franchisees would still have to pay for the regular wholesale price. As a result, each item sold during the Boxing Week Sale would cost the franchisees a loss of 30% of the retail price.

Many franchisors will require their franchisees to renovate their stores as a condition for renewing their franchise agreement. The reason behind this is that all the leasehold improvements may have been worn and torn. The store has to be re-renovated to maintain a good image of the franchise business. While most franchisors do this for bonafide reasons, some just make money from such schemes.

At least two popular franchise restaurant chains had a clause in their franchise agreements that required the franchisee to renovate their restaurant upon renewing the agreement. Their clause required the franchisees to hire the franchisor's designated contractor to do the renovation. The cost of renovation was often over $500,000. One of the franchisors actually used its in-house contractor to do the work and charged the franchisees a fee that was well over the market rate.

A Good Starting Point

Not all franchise businesses are profitable or practiced in a fair manner. On the other hand, not all of them are unreasonable or would take advantage of their franchisees. Some of the franchise businesses are excellent training platforms for people who want to be entrepreneurs but do not have the essential skills.

For example, you may want to open a coffee shop but know nothing about brewing coffee. You may take a barista course to learn how to prepare and serve coffee. However, the course will not teach you how to run a coffee shop from scratch. A franchise coffee shop may be a good training school to acquire all the techniques you need to possess as an entrepreneur.

Sometimes, we are misled by the scale of the franchise business, believing that the bigger the franchisor, the higher the franchise fee will be. That may be true in most cases, but some big franchisors may want their franchisees to start with a small store to prove the franchisees' entrepreneurial skills before giving them a big store to operate.

A popular retail franchisor had hundreds of stores. All their stores in metropolitans were big department-store style outlets with tens of thousands of square feet of storefront. Each of those stores had tens of millions of dollars in sales revenue per annum, so most people thought their franchise fee must be very high. While the franchise fee of a small coffee shop was around $500,000, the franchise fee of such a department store should be at least $3M. However, their initial cost, including the franchise fee, was only set at the $100,000 level with the franchisor's assistance, such as consignment sales and financing. It was because what the franchisor most wanted was the franchisees with excellent retail management skills and experience, not their franchise fees. A new franchisee would be given the opportunity to open a small store in rural neighbourhoods with only hundreds of square feet of storefront. If they could succeed in the small store, they would be given a bigger store in a bigger town. Step by step, eventually, the franchisee would be able to own a full-function department store. Such kind of franchise is an excellent choice for some entrepreneurs who have no innovative ideas.

9. Feng Shui

A bright office with natural light can raise the work efficiency of the employees and can reduce depression. Painting a room in red can make you feel warm while painting a room in white can make you feel cool. A coffee shop with the aroma of coffee beans can increase people's desire for coffee. A bank will only put its safe deposit boxes at the back of its branch instead of the front area. All of these practices make sense and are 'natural' feelings. They are, in fact, part of Feng Shui practices. Knowing how to practice Feng Shui, in general, can increase the productivity of your employees, the traffic of a retail outlet, the sales volume and, eventually, the profit of your business.

What is Feng Shui?

Feng Shui is the Chinese name for geomancy. It is a system of aesthetics with well-developed theories, using geographic features, figures, directions, and laws of nature to improve life. The fundamental theories include balancing the opposite characters of things – Yin and Yang, and the five elements – Wood, Fire, Earth, Metal and Water. Its theories rely on Heaven (astronomy) and Earth (geography) that cover everything human beings have to deal with, both tangibly and intangibly, known and unknown to us.

Feng Shui means literally "Wind and Water" in Chinese. Wind can mean air currents, rain, snow, sunlight, sounds, magnetic fields, electromagnetic fields, infrared lights, radon gas, and more. Water can mean rivers, creeks, roads, highways, flows of traffic and more. Both can be tangible and intangible things and can also be something that may not be known to us. For example, people did not know anything about radioactive substances, invisible lights and ultra-high-frequency sound waves one thousand years ago, but these substances did exist at the time. Feng Shui is a study of how the environment affects people by statistics and theories that have been developed for thousands of years.

Feng Shui emphasizes the importance of the flow of Qi. Qi is frequently translated as "energy flow". It is a concept of circulation or movement of some tangible or intangible materials. Qi is in the universe, in the sky, on the earth, inside our homes and even inside our bodies. Qi can be good or bad; wind, light, infrared, radioactive substances, invisible lights, and ultra-high-frequency sound waves can all be Qi. Qi is brought by Wind or Water. We want to block the bad Qi or aggressive Qi, welcome good Qi and have a good circulation of Qi.

Yin and Yang

Yin Yang is a Chinese philosophy. Yin and Yang are two contrary forces (or fields) interconnected and interdependent in the natural world, and they give rise to each other in turn. When Yang dominates and eventually takes over the whole environment (100%), it will reduce its power, and Yin will overcome Yang to start another cycle and vice versa. However, the time length for each cycle is unknown and may not be equal.

For example, fire is Yang, and water is Yin. A piece of burning charcoal will consume all its contents (including water molecules inside) and become ashes. When the fire is extinguished, the Yang is gone, and the ashes start to absorb moisture in the atmosphere, and the Yin takes back control as the ashes cannot be burned again.

Chinese philosophy believes that Yin and Yang are always paired and have to be balanced. Examples of Ying Yang are:

Yin	Yang
Female	Male
Earth	Sky
North	South
Wet	Dry

Dark	Bright
Cold	Hot

Yin and Yang have to be balanced. For example, when the house is too cold, we have to turn on the furnace to warm it up; when it is too hot, we have to turn on the air conditioning unit to cool it down. When a house is too wet, you need a dehumidifier to take away the moisture. When your home is too dry, you need a humidifier to give some moisture to it.

When a place is too bright, such as a sun-drenched office facing west, you need some blinds to block the sun. When a room does not have enough light, you should consider adding a more powerful electric light fixture or simply changing the light bulb if possible.

A noisy place is disturbing, even if it is a retail outlet (the only exception may be a club with loud music). It would be best if you turn down your audio system's volume even if you think the music you play is popular.

The Five Elements

The concept of the Five Elements has been used in many traditional Chinese fields, such as astrology, traditional Chinese medicine, music, military strategy and martial arts. Its general meaning is Five Movements or Five Phases. Five movements are centre (earth), right (metal), left (wood), forward (fire) and backward (water). The five phases are sink (metal), wet (water), grow (wood), hold (earth), and heat (fire). In Feng Shui, they represent the nature of directions and the Flying Stars, too.

The five elements are interrelated, and there are two basic cycles – the controlling cycle and the nurturing cycle (Figure 1).

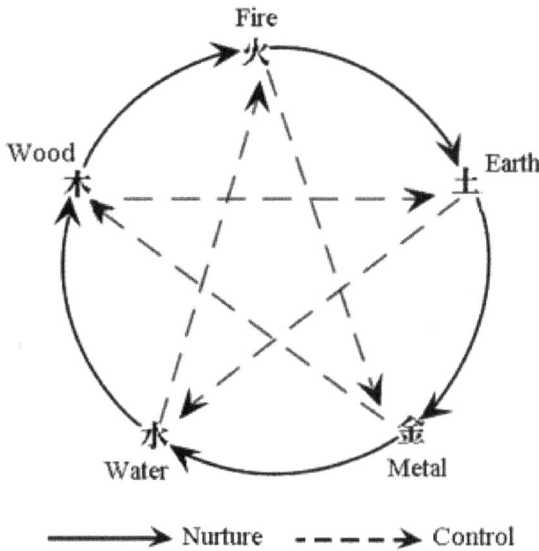

Figure 1

The two basic cycles of
five elements

The controlling cycle is explained by Fire melting Metal, Metal piercing Wood, Wood burdening Earth, Earth absorbing Water and Water extinguishing Fire. The nurturing cycle is explained by Fire making Earth, Earth producing Metal, Metal enriching Water, Water feeding Wood and Wood fueling Fire.

Whenever one element is too weak, or we want to boost that element for a particular reason, we may increase it by providing the same element or adding more of its nurturing element. On the contrary, when we want to reduce or control one element, we should avoid using such an element and should introduce its controlling element to the property.

While a Feng Shui consultant will use as many as four cycles and eight scenarios to balance the elements, the two basic cycles above explain the main theories of Five Elements. As a general rule, the five elements should be balanced in all premises. Each element has its representative and favourable colour as follows:

Element	Representative Colour	Favourable Colour
Water	Black, Blue	White, Silver
Wood	Green	Black, Blue
Fire	Red, Purple	Green
Earth	Yellow, Brown	Red, Purple
Metal	White, Silver	Yellow, Brown

Generic Office Layouts

It is impossible to set a tailor-fit Feng Shui office layout for everyone as different people, businesses, locations and orientations of buildings have different Feng Shui settings. However, there are some generic designs for general situations.

For a male's office, the door should be on the left-hand side of his seat, such as in Figure 2 below (as long as the door is on the left upper corner, it is okay).

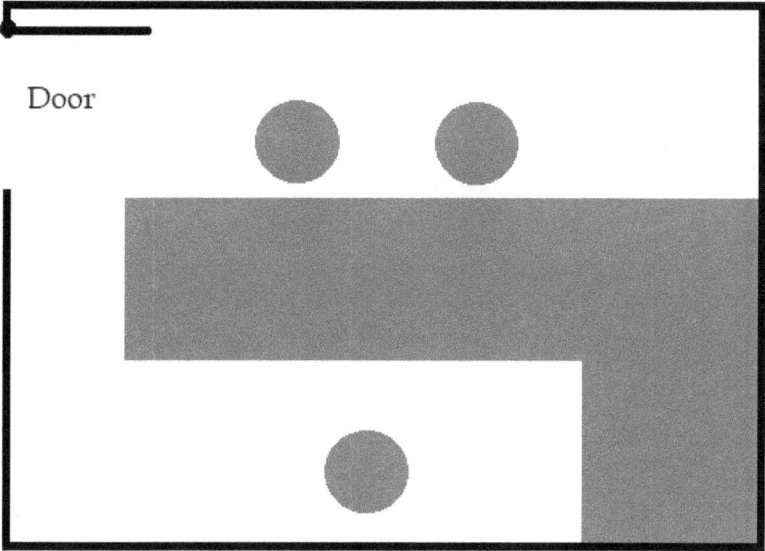

Door

Figure 2

A Male's Room Layout

For a female's office, the door should be on the left-hand side of her seat, such as in Figure 3 below (as long as the door is on the right upper corner, it is okay).

Keep in mind that no two doors of private offices should be opposite to each other. Otherwise, the occupants of the two offices will not get along well; hence, it is hard to have collaboration between them. The rooms of the management offices should not be in the front portion of the office. Never put your seats under a beam. Move them to a position that is not directly under any type of beam, including an air duct.

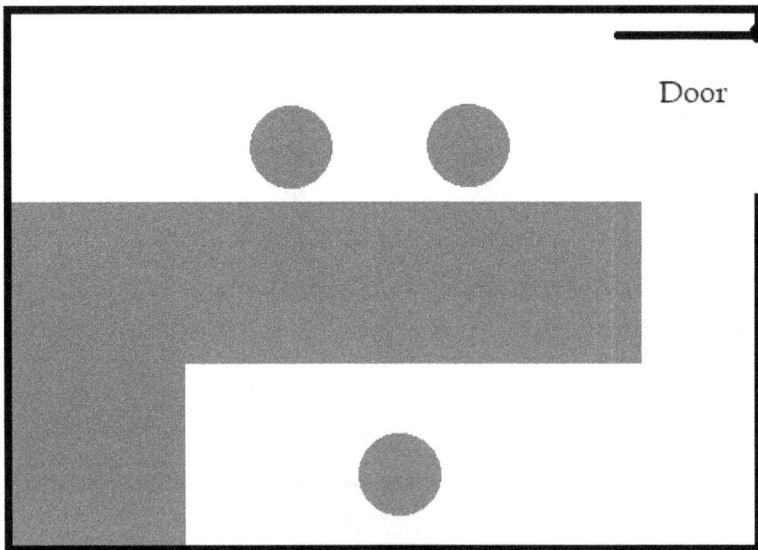

Door

Figure 3

A Female's Room Layout

Retail Setting

Traffic is a crucial factor in deciding whether a retail business will succeed or not. Higher traffic may provide more customers, but it may not always be true. High traffic does not mean that many people will visit your outlet and buy your products. That is why even a shopping mall is busy; some of its stores may still fail and close.

In most jurisdictions, their fire code or building code may require the entrance doors of retail merchants to swing in the direction of exit travel. That is, the visitors need to pull the door to the outside instead of pushing it to the inside when they enter the shop. This kind of door orientation makes sure that people inside the premises will not block the door from being opened in case of chaos created by a fire or an accident. However, which side the door hinges are installed on may affect the effectiveness of attracting customers to your outlet.

The entrance door of a retail outlet should be opened in the same direction as the traffic flow. If you are exiting the outlet and the traffic flows from the right to the left of the outlet, the door should be pushed open to your left-hand side. Figure 4 below shows the right orientation of the entrance door for that situation.

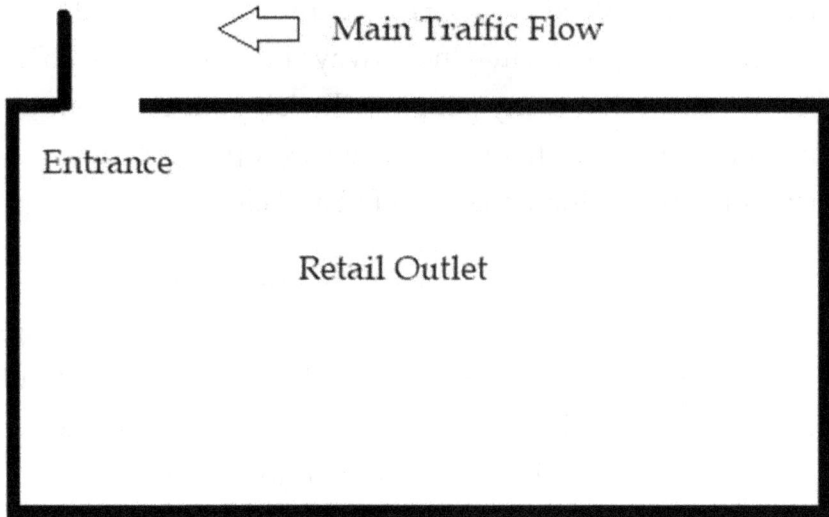

Main Traffic Flow

Entrance

Retail Outlet

Figure 4

The entrance location does not necessarily be on the left-hand side of the outlet, as shown above. It can be anywhere along the line. The only requirement is that the door has to be pushed open to the left when the traffic flow is from right to left.

When the traffic flow is from right to left, the door should be pushed open to the right (see Figure 5 below).

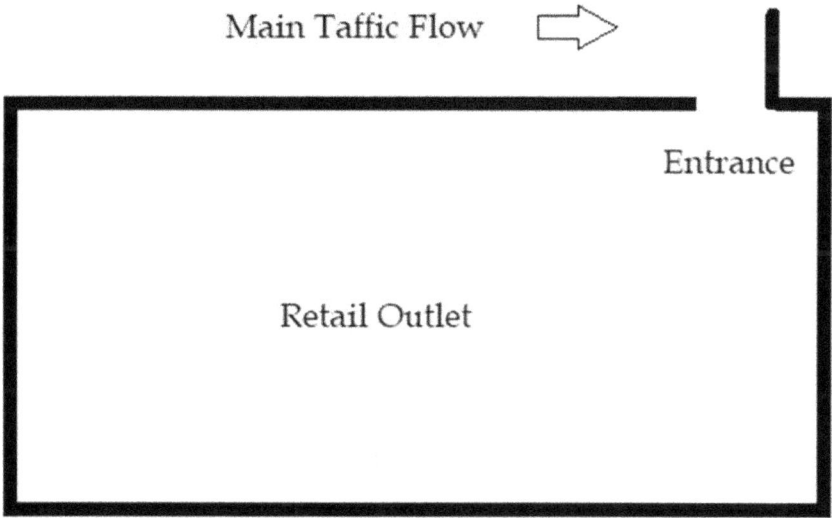

Main Taffic Flow

Entrance

Retail Outlet

Figure 5

If the entrance door is a double door, you should lock one of the doors to make it a single swing door to fit one of the above scenarios.

Feng Shui is not just a theoretical science; it has been supported and proved by billions of cases in China for thousands of years. Furthermore, the phenomena in Feng Shui may be explained by quantum entanglement, and both are subjects to be further investigated and studied. Having good Feng Shui can boost your business to a higher level. Good luck!

~ End ~

www.ingramcontent.com/pod-product-compliance
Lightning Source LLC
Chambersburg PA
CBHW070934210326
41520CB00021B/6936